WHY THE RIVER DISAPPEARS

WHY
THE RIVER
DISAPPEARS

poems by

Marcia Southwick

For Bob —
Many Thanks
for your clear insights
about these poems.
You've been a wonderful
critic + friend —
Marcia

Carnegie Mellon University Press
Pittsburgh 1990

ACKNOWLEDGMENTS:

American Poetry Review: "Boarded Windows," "The Body," "The Ruins,"
  "Small Difficulties," "The Sun Speaks," "Why The Rain Is Ignored."
Antioch Review: "Blood."
Cincinnati Poetry Review: "Arrest," "Finding Horseshoes," and
  "Voices from the Afterlife."
Field: "Child, Invisible Fire."
Iowa Review: "Doors Opening Here, And There."
Laurel Review: "The Gaze."
Mississippi Review: "Dolls," "Widower's Song."
Missouri Review: "Red Light, Green Light."
Ploughshares: "Solo."
Poet & Critic: "Fear Of Trains."
Prairie Schooner: "What The Sun Invents"
River Styx: "Brothers," "The Rain's Marriage," and "Why The River
  Disappears."
Western Humanities Review: "Poem Written After Finding My First Gray
  Hair."

"The Body" was reprinted in *The Pushcart Anthology*, Vol. 7; "Boarded
Windows" in *The Anthology of Magazine Verse and Yearbook of American
Poetry*; "Doors Opening Here, and There" in *Extended Outlooks:
The Iowa Review Collection of Writing by Contemporary Women*; and "Solo" in *The
Ploughshares Poetry Reader*.

"The Liar" first appeared in *Connecticut: Eight Poems*, a chapbook published by
Pym-Randall Press, 1981.

Six poems were reprinted in *Her Six Difficulties and His Small Mistakes*,
a chapbook published by Labyrinth Editions, 1988.

The author would like to thank the National Endowment for the Arts
for a grant which supported the writing of this book.

Notes: "The Afterlife," is for Stephen Tapscott; "The Visit" is for Shawn
Sturgeon. Special thanks to Jorie Graham and Hilda Raz for their help with the
title poem, and to Robert Pack for his advice and encouragement.

The publication of this book is supported by a grant from the Pennsylvania
Council on the Arts.

Library of Congress Catalog Card Number 89-61328
ISBN 0-88748-098-5
ISBN 0-88748-099-3 Pbk.

CONTENTS

for Nick

... Are we *here* perhaps just to say:
house, bridge, well, gate, jug, fruit tree, window—
at most, column, tower... but to *say*, understand this,
    to say it,
as the Things themselves never fervently thought to be.

—Ranier Maria Rilke—

I

THE SUN SPEAKS

I search for new meaning
and find black poplars
inaccessible like
locked doors, roses turning brown
from the inside out, and wind
that quickens into an almost material thing
as it nudges aside
a dry leaf here and there
to make room for itself. Shadows
shouldn't clutter the yard, but
they do. On a larger scale,
the landscape is further complicated by
a network of roads and sidewalks.
The entire pattern, seen from a distance, looks
almost life-threatening like
an underground root system. Yet,
on the subject of deserts and naked skin,
I'm still the expert. Who
really belongs here? I don't know. But
if the picket fence surrounding your house
seems less preoccupied than usual
and doesn't hold you in, take a long walk
to see the roses again.
If the night loses track of you,
along with everything else it obliterates:
back yards and sheds, for instance,
slipping out of existence as the night
erases things to perfection, don't worry. I'll be back
to stare down at you from my office of fire.

THE VISIT

On her way to grandmother's
she remembers the hurricane:
The electricity went off,
so they lit candles. The water rose.
From a distance, the lights in the house
must have looked eerie,
moving from window to window
in the pitch black.
The next day they heard
that several small boats
were lost at sea, found miles away,
splintered against rocks.
The coastline changed,
its sea wall battered. Trees
blocked the road. Where did the time go?
Now she's afraid of the woman,
who is bed-ridden and smells
like urine and sweat.
But she walks the path anyway
back to grandmother's house.
It's almost as though
a few yards away, a wolf,
its teeth bared, hides behind a tree.
She notices things decaying: trees
hit by lightning, and leaves
flattened, against the ground, by rain.
The place is so quiet that it's as if
the word *goodbye* will soon be whispered

just within hearing range.
Later, she almost says,
"What nice ears you have."
But her grandmother is asleep,
snoring like the wolf
the huntsman finally cuts open
to save Red Riding Hood,
who springs out saying,
"How dark it was!"—
glad to be free of the wolf's stomach:
it was pitch black inside
like a house with no lights
on the night of a hurricane.

DOLLS

If I were a doll,
brought alive by a child's
imagination,
and I were talking to you,
would you listen? "I've
got troubles.
Oh to feel the instant sadness
evoked by simple thoughts
of hospitals and rain!"
November pulls
down its yellow leaves.
It's good for us—
chaos and color, I mean.
Out in the street
I shade my eyes
to protect myself
from the sun's glare.
Then I remember a window.
I'd broken it with a red ball.
Into my last moment of
true ignorance,
my child's brain
still as empty as snow's,
the ball dropped,
shards of glass flying—
I was changed. I
drifted away from myself, as
adults do.
If I were a doll,

I'd turn my head—
"Isn't it time we spoke
the new language?"
Downstairs, deep in a cellar,
in my white dress and satin shoes,
I'd be speaking to no one.
Odd, I think, these
trees are odd.
Looking down as they do
into my white face,
my tangled hair.

WIDOWER'S SONG

Don't bones
matter to you? You
refuse to take back
your skin, refuse to wear
the blue dress
I loved so. You've left
your purse in the closet,
you've left your coat—
you won't need it as you walk
the new streets of heaven.
I'd think of snow,
but it's not worth it.
Drift after drift
keeps me apart from you
with walls of white. Rooms
surround me & mirrors
make me want to look at myself
for the last time.
"A woman can't make a watch,
she can only guess
it needs repair.
A woman can't find sticks,
she can only build a fire "—
proverbs meant to hurt you,
make you walk
up the stairs. I've never
wanted to see the shadows

shed their clothes.
I've never wanted to see
what's underneath. A dark
so dark is easy to love.
If snow doesn't touch you, and
you're protected, sealed off
by sky, your window, stare
down at me, through
clouds, those
indifferent ghosts.

FINDING HORSESHOES

When I forget grass,
summer exists without me. A boat
pushes away
from shore.   My name is—
let's keep it impersonal—
Nobody.   Are you the woman
falling through the floor?
It's none of my business.
The horse kicked up its hind legs.
I didn't suspect anything.
But then I looked on the upper shelf
and found the horseshoe.
Evidently, the silence had lasted too long,
and the cold had occupied the countryside in vain.
Horses had run away
and now the ice would rather be crushed
than feel so useless. So go ahead,
disappear without a trace.
Hurry, though, for this is a desert
where horses once lived.
Get a grip on yourself. It's the intention
of time to terrify you.
You wonder if boxes will arrive
filled with air you exhaled
on the day you were born.
Are you the woman falling through the floor?
The room doesn't see you
as you get out of bed.
Another day tracks you down,

almost as though by scent.
You ask yourself: Which direction
is the wind coming from?
The window looks out upon
a patch of weeds. The dog is crazy
and barks at shadows.
The furniture doesn't hide
the blank backs of walls.
And who are you anyway,
the wife of grass, of deserts where
horses once lived? A boat
reaching the other shore carries the news:
You've opened a box.
You've found another horseshoe,
the one given to you for luck
on the day you were born.

VOICES FROM THE AFTERLIFE

I'll give you the flowers, but
you'll have to find your own rain.
Sew the patches of silk together. Say nothing.
Kiss the statues goodbye. Blow the candles out
and cut the cake. Lie down.
Are you a saint yet?
Don't gaze at me like that, your mouth open.
This string tied around my finger
helps me remember to. . .
Everything is just as it was
back then. I'd say riddles like:
What did the angel see in the mirror?
Answer: nothing but it's own voice, a thin flame
burning without heat. It's too late
to start again. Threads are cut.
A coat falls apart, hem first.
Someone pretending to be a tailor
razor-blades the button holes.
The collar falls off. In this light it's hard
to distinguish between the fuzzy shapes of things:
Are the trees on fire, or is that a sunset?
What if the sun is fragile,
a round piece of paper burning?
Now you can hold your face up to the rain as if for
                                    inspection.
If the afterlife is a cold street,
look both ways before
going back to the house where you were born.
Watch for doors that shut you out. Watch for. . .

My mind is as clear as a pond
in which no drowning has ever occurred.
The bottom is false, like a trap door.
Don't gaze at me like that, your mouth open.
Here trees turn to ashes and the sky
stares over it all, mindless. . . .
Haven't you had your fair share of light?

RED LIGHT, GREEN LIGHT

The woods lock them in.
Leaves click
shut around them,
the children playing
Red Light, Green Light.

"What should I do?"—
a few words
drifting through my window
are loud enough
to halt the children's voices,
which vanish like
snuffed-out stars.

Pushing me back in,
holding the door ajar,
she said, "Stay here.
Here." Don't move,
there's an overflow of woods.
Or sprouting from
a crack in the floor,
the light, and four walls
sealing me in.

She shoved me back
into my body, a door
slamming, *"There,*
remember *this."*

It's the way the wind stops, and
the children playing
Red Light, Green Light
scatter forward.

The one who's *It*
says *Red Light*,
her voice a sliver of white ice
ringing the air.

HORSE ON THE WALL

She deserted you,
the aunt who sang you to sleep.
On your birthday years ago,
she gave you a figurine,
a blue china horse
that broke as you dragged it
across the floor. At five,
you felt the twinge you'd later recognize
as guilt. So here you are,
thirty-three years later,
standing on a street corner,
looking for answers:
It's evening and the first stars
will soon spot you
waving and calling to your friend
who wants to quit writing poetry
but can't. He should have stopped
his car for you.
You hear yourself
call his name again,
and the shock of it is like
the screech of tires rounding a corner.
Maybe you've just called
a name into history,
your voice flying past the great poets,
who lean out of doorways
into the gray rain. Unheard,
a call like that cannot turn back

and loses itself among the vacant
parking lots and side streets.
It's the way your aunt
must have disappeared, leaving you
awake at night, your mind
patching together bits of shadow
into a figure that looked like
a flattened version of the china horse
galloping on the wall.
Maybe your friend,
without a poem in his head,
adjusts the rearview mirror
and sees his own face
staring back at him like a stranger's.

BROTHERS

In a story called
"The Poor Boy in the Grave,"
the master says, "I'll be back
in five hours. If the straw
isn't cut in half by then,
I'll beat you senseless."
Your older brother is like that.
He locks you out of the house
and throws your French book
out the window. Later, Mother
finds you studying beneath
a street lamp. The next day,
after you've failed the test,
he twists your arm behind your back.
Mother won't be home till four.
You can feel his hot breath on your neck
as he pins you down
on the slick cement,
your face pressed against the cool
basement floor.
The boy in the story
cuts the straw, but by mistake
also rips his coat.
Afraid of what his master will do,
he swallows a jar of poison.
But you kick and scratch,
scurrying away. You run upstairs,
through the kitchen, overturning chairs
behind you as you go,

worried about what Mother will say
when she opens the door and sees
the mess: ripped curtains, plates
tossed, and chairs that look
like kindling— her face
frozen in shock. You think of the poor boy
half-drunk on poison,
stumbling over roots and stones in the cemetery,
looking for an empty grave
to leap into.

II

POEM WRITTEN AFTER FINDING
MY FIRST GRAY HAIR

A horse gallops away,
ahead of its own dust.
The sky wears
black rags. Grass
is flattened by hooves.
"The mouth is a hole.
Why doesn't it hurt
like a cut?" my son says.
We're lost, but
calendars will find us.
October fourth.
The night swallows
everything, even an ant
crawling across the floor.
The day my son was born,
it snowed, yet the snow
melted so quickly that
the streets stayed black.
That's as far
as my mind would go.
I imagined a child, but
I couldn't imagine him.
Separate parts
of his body moved,
pressing against my ribs.
He says, "Why is a table
called *table*, why
is a chair, *chair*?"
Backing out of the driveway,

31

one icy morning
on the way to his school, our car
swerved, taking us
across the neighbor's yard.
I saw myself from a new perspective
of apple trees
about to be hit. My son
and the birds watched me
as I straightened the wheel,
my first gray hair
the color of dust kicked
from a horse's hoof.

THE LIAR

Years ago I hid beneath the porch of our white
                                        farmhouse,
hoping that someone would notice my absence.
For hours I tolerated the ants crawling over my legs
because I wanted to hear my parents call out my
                                        name
in worried voices.
Nothing happened.
My mother and father sat on the porch above me
and talked about setting traps for the mice
that invaded the house each spring.

Once I painted a black half-moon beneath my eye.
At school I told a story that changed as the day wore
                                        on:
I had fallen from a tree,
I had been chased by my brother with a stick,
I had been slapped in the eye by my mother.
Soon the black eye seemed so real to me
I didn't notice the black paint
beginning to smudge across my cheek.
Of course, no one believed me.
But the stories were true and the paint was simply an
                                        excuse
to tell them.

My mother had migraine headaches and used to slap
                                        our heads
to ease the pain.
Sometimes she chased us through the house

with a pair of scissors in her hand.
Later, when my eyes went bad, I was relieved
because I thought the doctors would finally discover
                              my concussions.
But my mother wouldn't let them test me.
She didn't want anyone to know.
Now my mother claims not to remember any of this.
Either she is a mad woman
or I am mad, and this story is a lie.
Maybe it doesn't matter.
It only matters that something irrevocable happened,
causing me to say all of this.

FEAR OF TRAINS

"Blue and white china plates
are connected to the word departure, also to:
yellow flowers, the sound of
trains,
and the sensation of trying to read
everyone's lips through closed windows.

Often I'm afraid that windows
will be shattered by plates
like the ones Mother hurled after she read
Father's letter, when he went to
California by train
to live with a distant relative we hadn't heard of.

Then we moved to the outskirts of
town. Mother sat for days at the window
while out back, at the edge of the yard, I played by
                              the train
tracks, among the sunflowers, the yellow petals large
                              as plates.
I thought Father would be coming home soon, so I
                              listened to
the approaching engines, but I hid in the reeds

when they passed, afraid that Father would see me.
                              Mother read
Town and Country and *House Beautiful* and never
                              tired of
rearranging the furniture. She wanted to
change things, buying new curtains for the windows

and new sets of plates
for the table.

Sometimes, it's as if my train
of thought becomes a real train
in which Father sits and quietly reads,
separated from the rain and me by plate-
glass. When I think of
him, he puts down the book and stares at me through
                                    the dirty window,
his mouth partly open as if about to

say something. But I'm unable to
hear anything but the train
about to take him to California. People are waving
                                    from windows
heads are nodding in sleep, and eyes are closing over
                                    unread
magazines. Around me, voices talk loudly over the
                                    sound of
engines. Then I hear the plates—

Just as I am trying to read
my father's lips, he shouts to me from behind the
                                    window.
The train, departing, sounds like hundreds of
                                    shattering plates."

SOLO

There are times that falter
like flowers in front of me,
and times that take root in my chest
like a change of heart.
Certain kinds of foliage respond to me.
Ferns, for example, are onlookers.
There are also flowers that have died
only to be born again like old opinions.
Perhaps it's true that my body
won't always travel solo
away from the place of my birth.
I have come a long way
through the serious underbrush
and will probably come to a clearing soon.
I can't help thinking, though,
of all the shadows I've left behind
that were once very important to me.
It would be useless to look for them now,
the way it would be useless to keep track
of my footsteps lost in the grass.
And though I would like to be grass,
which doesn't defend itself
but simply waits to become undeniably green,
I know that there is nothing left to negotiate.
The old roads that used to lead somewhere
are now overgrown with weeds
and the sun aches to occupy everything.

THE BODY

In the future, there are ashes that control me,
and yet I go on troubling the grass with my footsteps.
I am reminded that this is a place,
and that my body will never learn to speak
the pale language of the sun.
I am reminded that the light of each day
will not pass through my personal history
to clarify the events that have changed me.
The night is obligatory,
and there is no point in trying to investigate its origin
in order to alter the state of things.
Outside, the blackbirds will always peck at the seeds
on the tough, brown lawns,
or disappear, without worry, into the sky,
which makes me think that the sky must be pure
as a future without sins,
and that one day I would like to go there too,
and be clear and shapeless, without belongings,
because I have had enough of my body
that surrounds me with its blood, hair, and teeth.
I have had enough of this autumn,
which is destined to fail,
as if the leaves contain within them the instructions
for falling, or as if they will whirl into next month,
unamazed at the new season.
If it weren't for me,
the coming night would be a chemistry of perfect shadows.

And as I walk into the open field,
I feel that the shy grass doesn't understand
what it is like to be of solid weight and mass,
to take up space, and to shiver in the cold.

BOARDED WINDOWS

Will I die while thinking of
dull gray houses in the rain,
attics where moths eat our clothes,
closets where mice sleep,
drawers that won't open,
doors that have lost their knobs,
newspapers piled in the cellar,
or faded yellow wallpaper?
Will I die while thinking of
apples rotting on the kitchen table,
dull knives, rattling pans,
rugs asleep in the hall,
shoes thrown in the corner,
or red curtains pulled shut?
I don't want to die in the silence of
floorboards waiting for footsteps,
old coats waiting to be worn,
mirrors waiting for eyes to look at them,
or flowers on a table waiting for water.
I don't want to die
because death reminds me of an abandoned secret
wanting to be told.
The secret is
nothing can alter the sequence of events
that have led me to make certain wrong decisions.
The secret is
the wrong decisions will crowd around me in the end
like apologetic children

trying to convince me of their good points.
The secret is
my past will seem suddenly less habitable
like a quiet house with boarded windows.
And so, I will refuse to think.
I will simply be aware of the rain
falling into the empty street
when I feel my body being pulled,
as if by gravity,
toward the end of things.

SMALL DIFFICULTIES

Is there any difference between what I am thinking
and the falling snow?
The snow is covering what I will soon forget:
the dry wheatfields, the pale leaves scattered everywhere
like small mistakes,
and the red house on the hill
where the neighbors sleep too soundly, like lovers
who haven't yet considered each other's faults.
To the snow, my footprints are small difficulties
to be taken care of later,
my breath and the cold air are a contradiction
of terms, and these words are like bird cries
that clutter the air for a moment, then die.
If it's true that I exist
in the shadow of my doubts that have appeared, like bad
                                            weather
out of nowhere,
then this would explain why I feel like timber
about to be cut down.
It would explain why there is something not quite right
about the ice on the pond,
which seems to give off a feeling of good intentions
even though it is dangerously thin,
and it would explain why the light of the moon outwits me
when it fails to enter my bedroom window
on the nights I wake from sleep and need to know
exactly where I am.
It would also explain why tomorrow, as it comes closer,

seems to have the look
of already having been lived in.
And yet the sun still bothers to rise and set
over the dark barns and fields of disinterested cattle,
as if to reassure them that they are still there.
So perhaps it's true that not all is lost.
The snow as it falls is repeating itself.
Over and over, it repeats what it is.

ARREST

As I write this, I imagine the police
standing over my desk, inspecting
each image, looking
for blood, knives, photos of victims,
evidence to arrest me.
They find only bare trees,
and wind that shifts for no reason,
discarding its details: stray twigs,
feathers, and bits of white paper.
The plum tree's branches,
half-blackened by fire blight,
form a lattice through which the sky
appears in fragments held together
like pieces in a puzzle.
Autumn has begun to make itself visible
by taking the shape of dead grass
and dried flowers. Then the police arrive
interrupting the clock, which ticks, halts
and ticks again.
For a moment I imagine the future:
rusted gutters fill with snow
as the night arrives, graver than usual,
wanting to take me by surprise;
silence takes the shape
of cabinets painted shut;
and mirrors, as if annoyed
by the sight of me, add another furrow to
the reflection of my forehead.
Then I open a door,

giving the shadows a chance to escape.
My senses isolate me,
causing me to wonder if I hear
my own footsteps
correctly: on the stairs, they repeat,
you walk, you walk.
I want to follow their echo,
leaving my body behind.
Why is nothing final?
The season continues to change,
reducing itself to its simplest form:
the first, falling leaf.

WHY THE RAIN IS IGNORED

The rain on the roof doesn't understand how
                              complicated
our memories are,
how we can choose to remember a hot day
in Moscow,
and the faces of two peasants quarrelling over a
horse,
but not the room of a hotel
we spent an entire winter in,
nervous or drunk.
Maybe we don't want to remember the day
we saw two lovers quarrelling.
It was November,
and the elm trees around them seemed unaware
of the words flung, like black coins,
into the snow.
So we concentrate only on the flaw
in the thin layer of ice on the pond behind them,
and try to forget
that one of them hurried over the surface,
as the ice creaked
with the sound of a pine tree about to fall.
Once, I stood in a spring fog
after hearing the news of your disappearance.
I can't recall exactly how I felt,
but the jonquils on the lawn seemed uncomplicated
as they tipped their heads
in the sluggish, gray air,

and a few pink blossoms fell easily from the
                                    magnolias,
as if the trees were unafraid
of their own nakedness.
Maybe we are part of a long story
to be told by someone who will purposefully
                                    misinterpret
what has happened,
so we shouldn't worry about the details of our lives.
It won't matter, finally, if we die
in a yellow field,
feeling the distance grow between ourselves and the
                                    flowers,
or in an empty street
beneath the neon sign of a bar,
in the silence just before someone touches the ivory
                                    keys
of a piano.
When we die, we do not reach conclusion.
In the minds of others
the memories of us will be altered.
Or we will be ignored,
like rain falling through the open windows of a house
where no one lives.

III

DOORS OPENING HERE, AND THERE

.

A broken rainspout.

A dream: water rising up the stairs.
Mother and I trapped in a small rectangular room.
Her bones turning to plaster
when I touch them.

A melon rotting on the kitchen sill.

Doors opening here and there into rooms
where no one is permitted.

Mother pushing Father away
without the use of physical force.
She looks at him as if from a great height,
the way one would look at stones on the ground
from the point of view of a roof.

All of this occurring over cups of coffee.

A few clouds scattered like minor complaints.

*

Mother's description of my brother's apartment:
no chairs, cardboard nailed over the windows,
and a wife who cries
when he returns from work and watches T.V.
without speaking.

Her possible description of me:
How one morning my son carried handfuls of ashes
out of the dead fire
and rubbed them into my hair as I slept,
stretched out, hung over, on the white couch.

Open windows. The wind disturbing the stillness
of the lamps and portraits.

The feeling of being lost among familiar objects,
of being unrecognized by the striped wallpaper
and dried flowers.

*

My husband in a closed room listening to Pachelbel.
In tears because his father, now dying,
used to close himself in a room and listen
to Pachelbel.

A crack in the wall that never shows itself.

My husband's father asleep in a chair
in the blue living room in California.
The wrong words that seem to seize him:
"How will you get there,
the four-lane hospital?"

The calm white of the almond trees.

The rain speaking in extinct syllables.

Connecticut. What Mother said to Father
about his change of career:

"I married a doctor, not a sculptor."
Father was measuring the distance
between my hairline and my chin.
For the bust.

What Father said to me
on a ferry from Maine to Canada:
"Your mother's friends play golf.
I hate golf."

                    *

Noticed the apparent closeness of a couple
walking down the rainy street,
just beyond the neatly trimmed hedges.

Then realized the rain was responsible.

Not their emotions but the rain
causing them to huddle together
beneath the black umbrella.

No comfort in knowing the trees have flowered
according to my belief that they would.

A few blackbirds jarring the ear with insults.

WHY THE RIVER DISAPPEARS

I can speak now.
Far from here, the Connecticut River floods
backyards and is guilty of nothing.

In places, the river eddies backwards, barred by rocks
or petrified trees

to where my mother says, "You know the bargain
gravesite by the river? We'd get our feet
wet, but I think we ought to buy it."

I imagine the water rising,
pushing itself up
onto my parents yard and over the lawn chairs,

but in real life, the water is calm.

My mother bought the bargain gravesite.
That was before my son could say, "Why do trees
have nothing to do, aren't they bored?"

Memory pares itself down.   A river as it ages
obliterates its own bends.

The bleached skeleton
nailed to the wall of my father's office, looked
rooted there for good.

How can I explain? My mother's floral wallpaper
is perfectly cut,

so that one corner meets another
without a seam.
The green flowers join, half-leaf
to half-leaf, forming a whole,

but my father's office mirror makes the furniture
duplicate and reverse itself:
chair, table, mirror, table, chair.

*

The house was old and one of the wide
floorboards gave way beneath the grand piano.
Workmen hauled it out with ropes,

but that night I dreamed the piano slipped again
through a hole in the wall by my bed.
Someone trapped inside was plucking the strings.

The next day, I thought the nightmare was the
                                        piano's.

Sometimes mice in the walls
gnawed the plaster, and Mother said: "That's the
                                        wind."

My father explained bones I found on the roof:
"They're drying out.
I'm building a skeleton."

Later, a neighbor died, and I thought bones would fly
out of the grave, looking for my father
to piece them together again.

Here, in real life, the windows look
at nothing more complicated than a yard,

and snow falling, like bits of white paper.
The front walk, leading to a side street,
means nothing beyond itself.

I imagine my parents' garden: the wind stops
bending the roses.
A bronze angel

perched between stones,
and half-buried in uncut grass,
looks so real

that it seems to breathe. Then the wind
interrupts, like the light

I switch on to stop my son's recurring dream:

floral vines on the sheets come to life and wrap
tightly around his neck. He wakes up, crying out:
"Those are squeezer flowers!"

                              *

Whenever the Connecticut River bends,
the water rushes forward
in a kind of ecstasy, as if unaware of

its own end. Finally, the bends don't matter.
The river disappears anyway, into Long Island Sound.

Other things won't disappear:

Walking down the street once
I heard a fire truck's siren, and could calculate
how distant it was by tracing the sound back:

the sound turning, this way and that,
around the buildings to reach me.

Maybe I'm right. Whatever enters the mind
is refracted, as a ray of light
alters its straight path

in order to pass obliquely from air to water.

I remember spending long afternoons
watching soap operas. On *Another World*, Rachel
argued with her husband.

I didn't like to go outside.
At first, I walked for hours, downtown,

shopping for clothes. Then I'd only go half-way.
Mannequins stared at me through windows,
so I'd walk only as far as *7-11*

for cigarettes. Newly married, I didn't speak for days
I erased my own voice,

my mind going blank. Like a white river reflecting
                                        white sky.

Or like this snow
erasing the yard's dead leaves, each flake covering
a last dark spot.

BLOOD

We are living according to a deadline.
That's the only explanation I can find for the crowd
that surrounded the victim shot on the walk
outside the restaurant where I worked as a waitress
in Cambridge, Massachusetts, 1970.
Nervousness passed from face to face,

                                as in the game *telephon*
we used to play as children,
where someone whispered us a secret and we passed it on,
until the last person in the circle said it
and the secret changed.
                    At some point in history
we must have received the original instructions for living,
but they are lost now.
All the hand-written messages
that explained what the years can't tell us
have been torn to shreds, all of the explanations
as to why the years wear out.
                       His blood on the walk—
and I remember now that a two-year-old
leaned away from her mother and placed a finger
in the red pool near the man's head
as if she wanted to know how warm a dead man's blood is—
has nothing to do with my life now,
                       has nothing to do
with the way my mind cannot hold its attention
on what is directly in front of it: this fall,
the redbud I am planting in the front yard,

58

and my own two-year-old, who has taken the shovel
                              from my hands
and is trying to dig, his face turning suddenly serious
and persistent as a gray sky.
                    That day, I felt as though
I had walked out of my childhood, as out of a burning
                              house,
and into my twentieth year.
I was afraid of the body on the walk,
and I wanted to throw something heavy over it,
a coat, but the little girl's mother did.
                              All my past fears
seemed insignificant: the time my father and I
sailed out to a lighthouse in the Chesapeake Bay
across rough water and I was afraid
of the spray which flew in my face,
and of my father's laughter which sounded like nails
shaken in someone's hands,
                    or the memory
of trying to piece together a blue and white china vase
I threw in anger against the wall when I was five,
and the sudden fear I felt when the idea struck me—
as it struck me again at twenty, and now—
that the essential shapes of things can all be lost.

THE GAZE

Cracks in the street branch out
in arbitrary directions—
some pointing towards a lone dog's howl,
and others towards. . . .
Each drop of rain
connects, yet doesn't connect
to the whole onrush of sound.
"I don't like the sound of that,"
he says, facing you.
He looks at you too long.
There's a point at which his gaze
stops short of you, as if he's seen
one too many things—
ash trees, for instance.
Leaves are tossed by wind,
a force other than his own.
You imagine a roof flying apart,
shingles turning up at random
in strangers' backyards.
Are you at fault, or is a fault
a widening crack in the street?
A muteness, a blackness
at the center of his thoughts
pulls you in.
Every time he exhales,
it lets you go.
You find yourself in a strange body,

your own body, as it turns out.
You want to begin again.
You want to speak,
but when you do, it's as if stones
are thrown into ponds.
The ripple effect is maddening,
extremely so.
The first words to reach his ears
are wrong ones:
"Don't you think the trees
block the view?"
What you meant to say was this:
"My mind is an axe
that's already cut them down."
The ice almost visibly refreezes in your drink.
Dust settles in the house, as if
nobody's crossed the threshold in years.
Silence ties its knots,
tighter this time.
Beyond the kitchen window,
grass is scarce in places.
There's nothing
a gray sky shouldn't say,
nothing it should.

CHILD, INVISIBLE FIRE

One day, the bread knife wasn't a bread knife
                                    anymore,
and she held it to my throat.
She wasn't a child anymore, and I hadn't aborted her.
She passed, unseen,
through the wall of the house and stood
at the end of the bed.
The muscles in my throat twitched
and I turned over.
I don't know where she is now, I know that.
But I would like to remove the small splinters,
bandage the small cuts, stop
her confused blood
from flowing every which way.
I hate these days playing themselves out
like piano scales,
and the redbuds exercising their right to bloom.
Someone sensible should put a stop to this.
A long winter should be called for.
The word love is abstract, less real
than the slippery oil on the roads.
I walk down the road
to our old house and think we could have lived there,
we could have blessed the moths
that invaded the house each year,
we could have sat in the cool shade of the oak
and talked. But talk is abstract, unsafe,

a shore that deserts us.
What was it you said as we crossed the lake one day
in the rickety boat?
You wanted a fire to burn the trees on the other side.
You wanted approval.
You wanted vocabulary to be simple, like a child's.
But a child has a head and shoulders.
Now, as I enter the house, the feeling begins:
I am observed by the chairs
and the white walls.
The continuous dreaming,
done by the narrow windows,
has nothing to do with the view.
And outside, the empty street slides into place,

its only oblivion.

THE RUINS

I'd bury my face in my hands but
somebody has to do it,
set the records straight: the combs were hers, the
                                    razors were his,
and the naked wax doll with the head missing
was mine. I'll step away from the ruins into the sunset.
I'll take a match to the whole thing,
I'll throw it away, the paper.

In the old days, the sun
was stronger,
so full of ambition that it saw through pockets
and blindfolds. No more.
They've taken away birds, they've taken down rafters.
I'm on display, and the sun watches me—
that's wrong,
it's completely self-possessed.

What if I've become one with the rubble?
Do I matter less than splinters of glass?
Do I matter less than spaces where doors used to be?
A button I've lost turns up—
it's here in the ashes, and so are my old gloves.
Why do my hands cast shadows on broken white
                              walls?
A last bird cries, making a wild guess.

Here, nothing is private:
The dirt, camouflaged by scorched grass,

shows through in spots like
bare skin on a dead horse's hide.
A few more leaves are absent today,
and everyone knows it.

WHAT THE SUN INVENTS

This morning, the sun, as it rises, invents
a few yards, trees,
and you again at the back door,
coming home late,
until finally I am there,
surrounded again by clocks and dull knives
in the kitchen,
where first I hear the strange
weeping, then watch my hand
cover the sound flying
out of my mouth. Looking back,
I think that if I could reduce the moments
of your leaving to only one—
to the moment, say,
between a glass being thrown
and the sound of its shatter in the corner—
I could begin to see why certain houses
must be abandoned.
The floorboards creak, dust collects
on the window sills, dishes pile up
and shirts scatter across the floor.
Anyone living here
would want to move out
into the open air
to escape the gnats circling the lamp,
the rattling water pipes,
and the light that resists
entering this house

even when I open the curtains.
No one would want to lie down at night
in a moonless bedroom
where sometimes I hear myself speaking
in a hushed voice, as if out of respect
for the gauzy black shadows
draped on the tables and chairs.
This morning, I don't know why
I am this particular woman
who sleeps, wakes, and sips coffee
in the brick house at the end of the road,
or why each day the sun, as it rises, invents this
house,
the coffee, the sturdy table, the wicker chair,
my own body, and outside,
the front walk
which swerves left, as if it were searching
for the quickest way out of my life.

THE RAIN'S MARRIAGE

In an African folktale, the rain
falls in love with a blacksmith.
At the wedding, the downpour dies out
to a single stream, a column of water.
As the first drop touches soil,
feet appear, then legs, a torso, arms. . . .
The woman, waves of transparent hair
falling over her shoulders, is called
the *Water Bride* and doesn't fully lose
her identity as rain. Once,
I was certain of the boundaries between my body
and whatever it touched, as if
touch itself were a way of defining exactly where *I*
                              stopped
and the rest of the world began.
Then I lost the sense that I was hemmed in
by skin. My body felt like something loaned to me—
it might break, or dissolve to ashes,
leaving me stranded,
a pure thought without a skull to inhabit—
like rain falling into any shape that accepts it,
every hollow place made equal by its touch.
The mind of rain
contemplates even the smallest crack in the parched
                              dirt
where nothing will grow.

Why can't I fall effortlessly in love?
If I knew the exact place where my body stops
and everything else begins, I'd marry.
Like the *Water Bride*, I'd be unafraid,
though surely trouble would exist, as between rain
and a blacksmith's fire.

Carnegie Mellon University Press Poetry

1975
The Living and the Dead, Ann Hayes
In the Face of Descent, T. Alan Broughton

1976
The Week the Dirigible Came, Jay Meek
Full of Lust and Good Usage, Stephen Dunn

1977
How I Escaped from the Labyrinth and Other Poems,
    Philip Dacey
The Lady from the Dark Green Hills, Jim Hall
For Luck: Poems 1962-1977, H.L. Van Brunt
By the Wreckmaster's Cottage, Paula Rankin

1978
New & Selected Poems, James Bertolino
The Sun Fetcher, Michael Dennis Browne
A Circus of Needs, Stephen Dunn
The Crowd Inside, Elizabeth Libbey

1979
Paying Back the Sea, Philip Dow
Swimmer in the Rain, Robert Wallace
Far from Home, T. Alan Broughton
The Room Where Summer Ends, Peter Cooley
No Ordinary World, Mekeel McBride

1980
And the Man Who Was Traveling Never Got Home,
    H.L. Van Brunt
Drawing on the Walls, Jay Meek
The Yellow House on the Corner, Rita Dove
The 8-Step Grapevine, Dara Wier
The Mating Reflex, Jim Hall

1981
A Little Faith, John Skoyles
Augers, Paula Rankin
Walking Home from the Icehouse, Vern Rutsala
Work and Love, Stephen Dunn
The Rote Walker, Mark Jarman

Morocco Journal, Richard Harteis
Songs of a Returning Soul, Elizabeth Libbey

1982
The Granary, Kim R. Stafford
Calling the Dead, C.G. Hanzlicek
Dreams Before Sleep, T. Alan Broughton
Sorting It Out, Anne S. Perlman
Love Is Not a Consolation; It Is a Light, Primus St. John

1983
The Going Under of the Evening Land, Mekeel McBride
Museum, Rita Dove
Air and Salt, Eve Shelnutt
Nightseasons, Peter Cooley

1984
Falling from Stardom, Jonathan Holden
Miracle Mile, Ed Ochester
Girlfriends and Wives, Robert Wallace
Earthly Purposes, Jay Meek
Not Dancing, Stephen Dunn
The Man in the Middle, Gregory Djanikian
A Heart Out of This World, David James
All You Have in Common, Dara Wier

1985
Smoke from the Fires, Michael Dennis Browne
Full of Lust and Good Usage, Stephen Dunn (2nd edition)
Far and Away, Mark Jarman
Anniversary of the Air, Michael Waters
To the House Ghost, Paula Rankin
Midwinter Transport, Anne Bromley

1986
Seals in the Inner Harbor, Brendan Galvin
Thomas and Beulah, Rita Dove
Further Adventures With You, C.D. Wright
Fifteen to Infinity, Ruth Fainlight
False Statements, Jim Hall
When There Are No Secrets, C.G. Hanzlicek

1987
Some Gangster Pain, Gillian Conoley
Other Children, Lawrence Raab

Internal Geography, Richard Harteis
The Van Gogh Notebook, Peter Cooley
A Circus of Needs, Stephen Dunn (2nd edition)
Ruined Cities, Vern Rutsala
Places and Stories, Kim R. Stafford

1988
Preparing to Be Happy, T. Alan Broughton
Red Letter Days, Mekeel McBride
The Abandoned Country, Thomas Rabbitt
The Book of Knowledge, Dara Wier
Changing the Name to Ochester, Ed Ochester
Weaving the Sheets, Judith Root

1989
Recital in a Private Home, Eve Shelnutt
A Walled Garden, Michael Cuddihy
The Age of Krypton, Carol J. Pierman
Land That Wasn't Ours, David Keller
Stations, Jay Meek
The Common Summer: New and Selected Poems,
    Robert Wallace
The Burden Lifters, Michael Waters
Falling Deeply into America, Gregory Djanikian
Entry in an Unknown Hand, Franz Wright

1990
Why the River Disappears, Marcia Southwick
Staying Up For Love, Leslie Adrienne Miller
Dreamer, Primus St. John